T0193962

NAUGHTY
&
NICE WAYS
to
SPICE UP
Your
MARRIAGE

Naughty
&
Nice Ways
to
Spice Up
Your
Marriage

J.D. BALL

NAUGHTY & NICE WAYS TO SPICE UP YOUR MARRIAGE

iUniverse books may be ordered through booksellers or by contacting:

iUniverse
1663 Liberty Drive
Bloomington, IN 47403
www.iuniverse.com
1-800-Authors (1-800-288-4677)

Because of the dynamic nature of the Internet, any web addresses or links contained in this book may have changed since publication and may no longer be valid. The views expressed in this work are solely those of the author and do not necessarily reflect the views of the publisher, and the publisher hereby disclaims any responsibility for them.

Any people depicted in stock imagery provided by Getty Images are models, and such images are being used for illustrative purposes only.
Certain stock imagery © Getty Images.

ISBN: 978-1-5320-9948-9 (sc)
ISBN: 978-1-5320-9947-2 (e)

Library of Congress Control Number: 2020911520

Print information available on the last page.

iUniverse rev. date: 06/26/2020

CONTENTS

HONESTY

I'd like to share thoughts, fantasies and ideas that I've gotten over the years after interacting with many married friends and acquaintances. I've watched so many couples in my life struggle with being imaginative enough to keep it going and sometimes they miss or forget the simple things that can make life sweet again. My mind has been blown, often, at the lack of consideration I've heard from husbands and wives as they share about their partners. I've seen some successful marriages and I've seen far too many unsuccessful ones. It saddens me when I can see a couple who at some point said that they couldn't or didn't want to live without the other person, completely give up and allow their marriage to fall completely apart.

One party wants to fix it, but don't broach the subject because of the fear of rejection, or they overthink and believe it can't be fixed, the brokenness is too severe. I'm here to say, it's okay to have the conversation, nothing beats trying. If it's fails without a try, then you'd never know if it could've been repaired. I've also known divorced couples, who were still in love with their ex-husband/wife, but no one spoke up before the papers were signed, filed and finalized. Don't lose faith in your partner or the relationship that you've built and yes, those are two separate things – the partner and the relationship, although separate they go together. How? Your partner (husband/wife) has become flesh of your flesh, bone of your bone and you've become one after the consummation of the martial vows. The promise of loving until death due you part, in sickness and in health, forsaking all others, etc. is a concept that people today take far too lightly. The person you've chosen should be loved as you would love yourself and care for yourself. If you're hungry, you find something to eat to feed the hunger. As a married couple you're supposed to feed each other, whether it's natural food or with communication, but there should never one person in the relationship providing all of nourishment. Because that means the one doing all the feeding will eventually starve for attention or love and seek it from someone else or die to the relationship. As for the relationship, it's all that you've accomplished together, the life you've built. It's bigger and deeper than the eye can see. More often than not, one party in the marriage is a little more selfish and feels that everything should cater to their needs and wants and that's all that matters and it's so very unfair to the person doing all the giving. Then you wonder what happens when he or she stops trying. I'll tell you. They will either walk away or someone else will come along and give them what has been missing, the love and attention they crave to have with their spouse and then the marriage is completely destroyed. They've given all that they can and there is nothing left.

I've heard so many different statements, for example, "Happy wife, happy life!" This is a real and true statement, but wives don't forget to do things for your husband, to show that you appreciate him keeping you happy and don't be so crazy that he's losing himself trying to keep you happy. Another one that is true but is not well received and seems to contradict the first statement is, "I'm not responsible for your happiness or it's up to you to make yourself happy." Okay, this one is tricky, but for some people it is true. I recently watched a couple discuss this topic and the husband was doing all of these over the top things, to make his wife happy and when it all boiled down, she was still not happy (although the public thought they were perfect) and all of the over the top jesters (building a huge house without consulting her and throwing an elaborate party "for her" without her input) were actually for him. He never consulted her on what she wanted. So, they had several years of strain, because neither wanted a divorce, but they loss the communication factor, because the husband thought he could do all of these huge "gallant" gestures and all would be right, no other woman could lay claim that her husband had done these things for her and she should be honored and grateful that she had a husband who could and did. It stills goes back to he never once consulted her on what she truly desired. If he would have asked her, he would have found out she felt suffocated in the relationship and lost. His personality and presence were so huge she was drowning in the marriage and no one to understand that she needed a life vest to stay afloat. When he finally couldn't take her misery any more he literally told her to go, do whatever she needed to do to be happy and he also realized he was not doing the grand gestures for her and that what he was doing was still mainly about him. It was refreshing to watch and the honesty that they shared was so eye-opening. It also leads me to my next point.

Never lose yourself to make someone else happy. This will never work. Someone will always lose and unfortunately, it's the person who's sacrificed themselves, thinking, if I give him or her all of me, then maybe, just maybe, they will believe me when I say, "I love you". The hardest part with this is you can't make a person believe in love until they know what it means for themselves. This willingness to lose oneself to try to keep the relationship going can also be a mask for one's own insecurities. Why do I say this? Well, as a woman we can mask our true feelings a lot longer than a man can. Sorry, some may not like it, but it's true and I've seen several women do it. We can be in a relationship for years and never be in love. Oh, sure, we can justify why we're in it, but it's still not fair to the man we've made believe that he's our everything when in reality, he's just the guy who came along at a time she didn't want to be alone or she was ready to settle down and the man she really loves, is either not ready or he's in love with someone else. Today, many base their decision to love on lust or loneliness, not fully understanding that those two things will not make a marriage grow or last. Where will that leave you?

In a cold and lonely marriage with someone you're tolerating. This is also known as settling. Unfortunately, you can be married and still feel alone. Again, I apologize, but the truth hurts sometimes. It wouldn't be the truth if it always felt good, it may not feel good or go down well, but if you can keep it down, like bad tasting medicine, it can do what it needs to do, which is help you heal. Never settle, because the aftermath only puts you back in the state you were in before you settled, alone. If we're honest it's hard being in a relationship with someone you don't truly love. Life gives us enough twist and turns, so having an honest and pure love makes it so much easier to maneuver through. So many couples have run out of ways or ideas to keep the fire going in their marriage and decide to give up without a fight. In a lot of cases it can be going back to the simple things that made them fall in love in the first place. Then there are those who don't have the first idea of how to be romantic. Over the years I've heard a lot about relationships do's and don'ts, but never how to keep it fun and exciting. Even after being married for over 40 years my parents still not only love each other, but they like each other. I love watching them laugh and joke around and the kisses they just randomly give each other. People do not realize how important it is to like and love each other in a relationship. Days may and will come when desire isn't felt or one of you aren't in the "mood", you should still want to desire to be in the others company. Like and love go together when you're in a marriage, 'til death do you part, isn't that the promise that was made on the day you committed your lives to each other? In sickness and in health, is definitely one of those powerful love lessons, where your ability to care goes far beyond yourself. I'm not a professional; I'm someone who's picked up some valuable life lessons along the way. I've met quite a few men and women who were unfulfilled or unhappily married and unfortunately, they can't think outside the box enough to rekindle the fire. One thing I discovered in the conversations I've had with women is the brokenness or insecurities we as women have when we're in relationships that we mask with fake strength or fake confidence especially with our bodies. Embrace all of you, the good, the bad, and the ugly. No one is perfect, and no one should expect perfection out of you. It's okay if you're not Superman or Superwoman but be your true authentic self when you're in a relationship. Never allow someone to marry your alter ego. It's too much work and it makes the marriage harder when you're trying to prove you're someone you're not and the marriage will fail, or misery will ensue if the real you is never present.

Marriage is a covenant relationship that two people enter into when they've chosen their life mate. Corny, I know, but it's also very loving and sweet. Of the billions of people on this planet you've found that one person you can't live without nor do you want to. Within this union there are ups and downs, but you should never lose your imagination on keeping it fun and exciting. In case you have, I've come up with some simple, naughty and nice, yet oh, so fun ways to keep the spark and sizzle very much alive. It should never die that's what makes loving each other so much sweeter.

FOUNDATION

Let's start with friendship. To be able to withstand the down times you have to be friends. Who else is there when family isn't, real friends. Your husband/wife should be your friend first and foremost. We often find ourselves confiding our inner most feelings and secrets to our friends and that is why having that kind of open and honest friendship with your spouse makes your marriage grow and flourish. It's okay to have your husband/wife be your best friend. I recommend it. Your friendship is the foundation that your love for each other rests on. This is also how you get through those time when sexual desire isn't present. Cover each other in love and prayer, which leads into the next point.

Your marriage is sacred and should be treated as such. Praying together may seem like a cliché, but it solidifies and covers your union and you keep God in the forefront of your marriage. I know this may be an outdated concept to some, but I believe God is the source our strength when times get tough and they will, with Him you can't lose. Even if it's a quick prayer, before leaving home ask God to protect and cover each other throughout the day from any dangers and forces that will try to come against your union in any way. Do this with genuine sincerity each day. Your spiritual relationship is just as important as your natural relationship. No one fully understands the forces that we encounter each day that are unseen but having someone support you spiritually is so special. When all else fells you have someone, who will pray God's love and care over you when life seems to get too hard to bare at times. Understand the difference between Love and Lust. Even the dictionary shows us the difference between the two. Love is defined as an intense feeling of deep affection arising out ties of kinship or personal ties. Lust is defined as very strong sexual desire. Lust is only tied to sex and it's a feeling that can be had for anyone and to be honest it's only surface. There is no depth to lust. Once it wanes then you're left with nothing. Love doesn't have to be boring there is an amount of lust that must be attached to your choice in a mate, but it shouldn't be the main reason for your choice. There needs to a connection beyond surface, pass someone simply being pretty or handsome. I've met plenty of pretty/beautiful women and handsome men who have bad attitudes and it takes away from their outer/surface beauty. Don't get trapped by lust and mistake it for love. You can have chemistry (lust) with many people, but you get a real connection when you see beyond what is visible. Love is taking the time to understand the other person, beyond sex. The bible tells us best in this area, "Love is patient, love is kind. It does not envy, it does not boast, it is not proud. It does not dishonor others, it is not self-seeking, it is not easily angered, it keeps no record of wrongs. Love does not delight in evil but rejoices with the truth. It always protects, always trusts, always hopes, always perseveres. Love never fails..." (1 Corinthians 13:4-8a, NIV) There is no other breakdown of love that is better in my opinion. Don't get me wrong, sex is important in marriage, it should be a part of the house, but not the foundation the house (which is your relationship) is built on. Since it is an intricate part of the house let's keep it exciting and fun.

USE MY IMAGINATION

We don't have to keep ourselves so contained. There is nothing wrong with exploring your sexuality with your husband/wife. There are several ways you can spice up your relationship. Some ways are done with simple acts and others can be played out or staged in some way. Either way you can bring pleasure and fun at the same time to your relationship. I believe pleasure should be given equally, I don't think only women should have all the attention and rewards of being in a covenant union. I recall a guy telling me that men want romance too. This shocked me, I'd never heard that before. The following fantasies, acts, and suggestions will be ways to please your wife or your husband. This also keeps the balance and allows for the man to be romanced as well. Remember the marriage bed is undefiled, as long as your spouse agrees with your ideas or suggestions then have fun and enjoy each other (Hebrews 13:4 NIV).

Naughty Fantasy – Pleasing Her

You're sitting on the couch with nothing on. Just listening to music and reading a book. He comes into the room not making much noise and then he just stares while you continue to read as if he isn't there. Then he begins to move closer to the couch and instead of sitting he kneels in front of you and begins to rub up and down your legs and then he inches his way up your thighs and you put the book down on the table nearby and look him in the eyes as he continues rubbing his hands over you. You shift positions on the couch to where your legs are now in front of you, so he can have better access to all of you and your breathing picks up and so does his, because he can't help but to notice the hardening of your nipples and the scent of your sex. This turns him on even more. He leans in and kisses you on your lips and literally sucks the air from your lungs. His mouth is hot, and you can taste his passion and he smells of man. You grab his head and make sure he deepens the kiss even more. Your tongues begin dueling to see who would become the victor. Then he comes up for air and looks at the desire that's shining in your eyes and he kisses you again. This time you release him, so he can lick and suckle down your neck, you even angle you head back so he can get better access to your sweet spot, then he trails his tongue back up to your earlobe and you can't help, but to whimper out his name and then release a purr. His tongue is so wicked, and each sensual caress is driving you over the edge. He can't resist any longer your hardening nipples are beckoning, and he suckles your right nipple into his greedy mouth and sucks as if he's a newborn, while squeezing the other between his thumb and index finger. Then he applies the slightest amount of pressure to your nipple and instantly your legs open and he hand seeks out the hottest spot on your body. While suckling your breasts his hand is searching the folds of your intimate core and finds you hot and wet. He gently strokes your clitoris with very little pressure. The twin assault of his mouth and fingers are taking you under and fast. As his mouth moves to the left breast to pay homage, he inserts one finger into your core and slowly moves it in and out at a pace that is driving you insane. Then he realizes your need for release, but he's can't let you climax just yet. He has to taste what is driving him mad. So, he releases your breast long enough to pull you to the edge of the couch and open your legs wide and bury his face between your scented thighs. When his hot tongue latches on to your clitoris he begins to lick and suckle gently, taking extra care as not to hurt you. His objective is pleasure not pain. You're going out of your mind and you can no longer hold back the screams that erupt from somewhere deep inside. You arch forward to give him better access and then he tastes you as if he wouldn't be able to take his next breath without having you this way. Your legs begin that telltale sign that you're about to climax and your entire body quakes. Finally, he lets you explode, and he takes you to a place in the heavens that only he can take you. And as you make your descent he kisses his way back up your body and right before he kisses you on the lips he breathes how much he loves you…

Pleasing Her Note:

This will just be the start of your night. If being naked is not your thing ladies, then make sure you have on something that will catch his eye to get him aroused. No sweats or baggy clothing keep it sexy. It will be just as hot with him having to peel the clothing from your body and the results will be the same, you'll be very satisfied.

Naughty & Nice Fantasy – Pamper Him Night

Before your husband leaves for work that morning let him know that you have a special night planned for him. Explain that this will be a night about pampering and pleasing him. Your explanation will do two things. You've given him a great reason to come home on time and you're on his mind all day long. Remember, your pleasure will come from him being pleased. Some men want to make sure their wife has received her pleasure before them, but in this case, let him know that tonight will be all about him.

Your first step will be to instruct him to let you know when he's on his way home. You can accomplish this via text or phone call, so you can make sure the night goes off without a hitch.

When he arrives, he sees there's a note on the door with his name on it. He opens the note and reads the instructions.

Come inside and prepare to be treated like the King
that you are. Once inside, lock the door, because you
will not be leaving out again tonight. Move to the next
note on the table near the entrance.

Once he's inside he will notice the lights are off accept for the light on the table near the entrance, this will give enough illumination for him to read the next note, but there will be candles lit around the room near the entrance. He will take in the ambiance and then read the next note.

> *Place your things on the table and then proceed to remove all of your clothing, including your underwear and leave all clothing in the designated basket by the table. After you've removed your clothes. I want you to put on the robe hanging on the hook to the left of the table. Once you step into the hall, follow the roses into the master bedroom.*

Once he arrives in the bedroom he will hear smooth jazz playing low and see more lit candles all around the room. You will emerge from the corner chair where you too will have on a robe without any clothing on underneath. Approach him slowly and make sure you greet him with a warm smile and then open his robe and rub your hands over the upper part of his body. Just to reacquaint yourself with the warmth of his skin.

By this time, he's probably wondering what this is all about. Simply tell him that he deserves a night of pampering and you want to make sure he understands that he is loved and appreciated. Tie his robe back and once that is settled you reach up and pull his head down, so you can taste his lips. You breathe in his essence and it's all Man. You relish his taste; his kisses always make you weak. You take his tongue and suck on it as if it's what you need to nourish your soul. He takes control of the kiss and deepens it more. When he releases your mouth, you're looking into each other's eyes trying to catch your breath. Once your breathing has slowed, you lean up to take another lick of his lips before stepping back. You take his hand and lead him to the table you've setup in the bedroom for an intimate light dinner. (Keep on the robes, you will be removing them later.) After you've eaten, hand him another note you had hidden under your place setting at the table and then walk into the bathroom but leave the door ajar. He reads,

*Your dessert is waiting. Remove your robe and come
enjoy a long hot soak in the tub.*

When he enters you stand in the tub and hold out your hand
and ask him to step in. You sit and allow him to sit in front of
you. THIS NIGHT IS ALL ABOUT HIM. So, let him lean back
against you and allow him to basket in your embrace and rest in
your bosom. There is a table sitting near the tub with chocolate
covered strawberries and champagne (or sparkling cider for those
who do not drink alcoholic beverages). Share a toast and slowly
feed him the strawberries. Once the strawberries are gone ask him
to tell you about his day. While he's talking, lightly kiss his neck
and work your way up to his ear. Nibble there and then make your
way back down the back of his neck. This action may end anything
he's saying, but just in case be attentive and listen. When he's done
sharing ask him to stand in front of you and do not be surprised at
his arousal. You lean forward and take his already hard arousal in
your hand and begin to stroke him. Up and down, up and down,
up and down, while looking him in the eyes. Then when he least
expects it, lean forward some more and take a lick of the head of his
throbbing arousal, but never stop stroking. This will cause him to
shudder or moan, but know he's pleased. Then take one last look up
at him, smile, whisper "I Love You," then take him into your mouth
as far as you can. Allow the heat and wetness from being inside your
mouth to drive him mad. When you know he can't take it anymore
begin to pull him in and out, in and out, in and out of your mouth.
Then pull him out of your mouth completely and lick up and down
the sides and come back to the top and give him a long lick across
his slit and then take him in your mouth again. Suck until he calls
your name and tells you he can't hold back any longer. Then lock
your mouth on him, until he explodes.

Some men will attempt to pull out of your mouth, but if you
can keep him from pulling out do so. After he gets his breathing in
check give him a kiss on his trembling member and stand and get

out of the tub. Dry yourself a little in view of him and put back on your robe. He's probably staring at you strangely, but that's okay, let him know that was just the beginning and thank him for being your dessert. Hold out your hand again so he can step out of the tub and you take a nice fluffy towel and dry him from head to toe. Wrap the towel around his waist. Then take his hand and lead him back into the room and instruct him to lay across the bed for his full body massage. Turn your music up just a bit, remove your robe, climb on the bed and pull out your warm body oil you've had warming on the night stand and go to work on kneading out all his worries and cares. After taking special care of his back, down to his buttocks and even his thighs, make sure he feels your nakedness during the process. Now it's time to take even more care with his front, so you instruct him to turn over. This time you straddle him and begin to work your magic. As you massage him take time to lick him in all his sweet spots. Once you are sure he has been thoroughly rubbed down and you've gotten your fill of tasting his delicious body, you lean in for another one of his toe-curling kisses and allow him to guide his engorged member into your heavenly gate and breathe out how much you love him…

Pamper Him Night Note:

Keep in mind you can revamp this to your liking or to your man's tastes. This is only to get your imagination flowing. There are so many ways to make this night of pampering for him special.

NAUGHTY FANTASY – HELP ME WASH MY HAIR

"Baby, will you help me wash my hair?" I'm leaning in the doorway of the master bath and he's resting on the bed. He looks up and smiles his big dimpled smile and stands and begins removing his shirt. I stare as he reveals his sexy upper body. Then he reaches for the waist of his sweatpants and rolls them down his legs as he is walking towards me. My mouth is dry staring at this beautiful specimen of a man who belongs to me. All I see is smooth caramel skin, well-toned abs, thighs that shows he loves to work out and don't get me started on his beautiful manhood that is standing at attention. I look down and smile and ask, "Are you that happy to help me wash my hair?" He looks into my eyes and says, "Baby, I'm always happy to help you in any way I can." I straighten from my leaning position in the doorway and step into his waiting embrace. At his height of over six feet he leans down and swipes at my lips with his hot delicious tongue. I groan and slowly open my mouth to allow him entrance. He pulls me even closer, I don't know how that's actually possible, but he does, and I melt into him wrapping my hands around his neck. Our tongues are tangling, and he wants control, so I relinquish it to his masterful skills and just accept one of his toe-curling kisses. I can't believe I'm about to climax just from his kiss. When he releases my lips, so we can catch our breath I realize my hands are now sliding down his chest and I begin to stroke his left nipple and then I lean in just enough for my tongue to lightly lick his erected nipple. Then I begin to gently suckle as I rub the other. His breathing quickens, and I know I'm pleasing him, and I give the right one the same attention with my eager tongue and then I pull back to blow on it. He growls deep within his throat and lifts my head, so he can take my mouth again as he walks me backwards into the bathroom. He reaches down and begins to squeeze my behind while still kissing me. He knows I love it when he does that. My body is on fire and I feel my body trembling and my panties are wet. He breaks the kiss again, this time to step into the large marble shower with dual shower heads and proceeds to turns the water on full blast. As the steam begins to rise. I stand in the middle of the bathroom staring at this beautiful man and realize I still need to remove my tank and panties. When I reach for the helm of my shirt, he stops me and says, "Let me." With his warm heated gaze, he walks back over to me like a lion stalking his prey and when he reaches me he leans in for one quick kiss and slowly lifts my shirt over my head and drops it to the floor. Then he goes to his knees and pulls my panties down my legs. I hold his shoulders to lift my feet one by one to step out of them. He does the unexpected and leans in and inhales my arousal and kisses my mound before he stands. As we stand in the middle of the bathroom completely naked he tells me how beautiful I am as he strokes his hands over my body and says, "I can't wait to taste you." I shiver from his words. I reach out to run my hands over him and I feel him tremble.

It's hard to believe that I can make him feel this turned on. All he has to do is look at me and I'm a goner. Being loved by this man is unreal and amazing all at the same time. As my hands travel down his body, warmth spreads through me and I can't wait to feel him in my hands. I reach my goal and I realize how large, hard and velvety smooth he is, then I use both hands to stroke and rub his erection. He backs up against the wall and leans on it while I explore his arousal with my eager hands. As I stroke him with my right hand I use the left to run my thumb across the head and I hear his voice catch, but he doesn't stop my ministrations. Instead he's moving his hips in a way that's matching my stroking and I hear him say, "squeeze harder baby" and I do, and I'm drunk on being able to pleasure him this way. Then I couldn't take it any longer, I drop to my knees as the bathroom fills even more with steam from the running shower and I lick across the head of his member. When I feel him tremble again I get bolder and suck him into my mouth. He's stroking my hair as I stroke and suck on him until I hear him tell me to stop. I lift my head and look him in the eyes as my hands continue stroking him gently. He lifts me to my feet and kisses me so deeply I thought I'd pass out from the pleasure of his kiss. When he breaks the kiss, I know he can see the blaze of passion reflecting in my eyes as I can see it mirrored in his. He moves me to the double vanity sink and moves my chair, lifts me to sit in the middle and he pulls me to the edge and he sits in my chair and looks at me as if I was the most beautiful woman in the world and he begins to squeeze my breasts and then he takes the nipple of my right breast into his mouth and suckles on it until my nipple is hard as a pebble. I can't help but moan out my pleasure because of what his hot, wet mouth is doing to me. His other hand is rubbing and squeezing and pinching my left nipple and I'm squirming because he's about to make me climax sitting on the sink giving my breasts his most undivided attention. He then begins to kiss down my body to my belly and then he smiles and pulls me forward and spreads my legs and puts them over his shoulder and leans forward so he can devour my intimate core. The moment his tongue touches my clit I scream. This man's mouth should be outlawed. The way he glides his tongue up and down my lips and then delves it deep inside of me and does this circle motion. Then he does this gentle sucking at my clit and I come completely apart trembling and expressing my love for him. I feel him smile as he kisses his way up my body. He then stands back up and kicks the chair out of the way and leans in and kisses me so sweetly that I almost climax again. He positions his hardness between my legs and I can feel him hard and heavy against my clit and he rotate his hips just a bit and then I can feel him slowly sliding in me and the feel is so exquisite that I stop breathing until I know he's buried to the hilt. His head is thrown back and I can see the veins in his neck, so I begin to intimately squeeze him with my vaginal muscles and he trembles and looks at me with this fire in his eyes. He begins to move ever so slowly in and out of me. It feels so amazing that I feel a tear slide down my cheek and he leans in and licks it away and then he begins kissing me as he strokes me, and I release the edge of the sink to reach between his arms that are holding my waist to pull him in deeper and I begin to rub and massage his perfect behind. I know he's close because I am too. He does this rotation of his hips and hits my spot and I explode to the heavens. My body is shaking as if it will never stop and then I feel his hot release hit my womb and I groan in satisfaction and then he's kissing me again. After coming back to earth and my wonderful husband helps me down from the sink I smile up at him on weak legs and tell him, "I still need to wash my hair." He laughs out and leads me over to the shower and we let the water wash over our sweat drenched bodies and it begins to wash away the loving we'd just experienced. There was more to come, my baby begins to pour shampoo in his large hands and instructs me to hold my head back while he lathers and massages my scalp. When he finishes massaging in the shampoo. He put me back under the water and the shampoo just cascaded down my body and once the water is running clear he repeats the process once more. Then comes the conditioner. I tease him about being thorough and he winks and says, "in all things" and all I could do was smile up at him. He leans in for a quick kiss. I look back up at him and let him know how blessed we are to have each other. He pulls me closer and says he feels the same way. I then reach up and pulled his face down to mine and kiss him my way, with all the love I have in my heart. When I break the kiss, only because we need to breath we know the night is far from over. He puts me back under the water to rinse the conditioner out and it was a good thing too because the water was starting to turn cool. He turns the water off and we stepped from the shower. He grabs two towels one to wrap around me and the other to wrap around my head. Then he grabs another towel for himself and he proceeds to take me back into our bedroom...

Help Me Wash My Hair Fantasy Notes:

Who would have thought asking for help to wash your hair could lead to so much satisfaction and then some? Yes, this is a task you can do on your own, but why not have some fun doing it. Imagine what other simple tasks he can help you with. And men if you did not realize it, kissing is important, it's extremely intimate for a woman.

NICE GESTURE –
CALL HIM JUST TO SAY

He's at work and so are you, but you'd like to make sure you're on his mind. So, when you decide to take a break pick up the phone and call him and make sure he's able to talk. Most likely he will have a second and that is all you need to tell him why you called. Here's where it gets fun, regardless of how you sound, begin singing to him the chorus of Stevie Wonder's song, "I Just Called to Say I Love you".

"I just called to say I love you,
I just called to say how much I care,
I just called to say I love you,
And I mean it from the bottom of my heart."

Then blow him a kiss, tell him you love him, and you'll see him when he gets home and disconnect the call.

Call Him Just to Say Notes:

This action serves a few purposes.

1.   Men need romance too.
2.   If his job is stressful, it will make him feel some relief and put a smile on his face and he's happy about coming home

and may leave work early just to finish what you started when you called.

3. If there's someone trying to get his attention, then he's reminded of what he has waiting for him at home. Always be the one to tell him how much he's appreciated and loved, so if he hears it in from a stranger it will be of no effect.

NAUGHTY FUN FANTASY –
SATURDAY SURPRISE

If your man works out or even if he's just relaxing around the house, surprise him with a quick and totally unexpected hand job. Yes, I said it hand job. The part I like about this one is you get to be the initiator when you come up on him from behind and give him directions on what you'd like him to do. If he's not walking by, then call him to you. Ease up on him and lead him over to the wall. (Put a towel down, just in case.) Then have him put his hands on the wall. Then you ease your hand around his midsection and slowly run your hand across his stomach and then move your hand around to his back and run your nails gently up his back. (Shush him if he starts to talk, let him know you want to play.) Then run you nails down his back and move your hands to the front to unbuckle his pants and if he's wearing sweats or shorts without a button and zipper, even better, then you just slide them down his legs. No underwear, great, if he's wearing them then ease your hands down the back of them and squeeze his behind as you lean in and give him a nice wet open mouth kiss on his back. Then ease the underwear down his legs. Let him keep his pants and underwear (if he has any on) around his ankles, this way he can't move from what you're doing, and he has to absorb the pleasure you're giving him. Make sure you run your hands up his legs when you stand from lowering his pants and underwear. Try not to disconnect so he can continuously feel you. As your coming back up squeeze his sexy behind again and then move your hands to the front and begin to stroke his growing arousal and keep applying pressure as you move your body closer to his as you stroke him, up and down, up and down, up and down, until his explodes. As he's trembling from his release give him one last open mouth kiss on his back. Clean him off and then pull his pants and underwear back up. Turn him around and then lean in for a passionate kiss and tell him he can continue what he was doing, wink and walk-off. Let the rest of the day unfold…

Saturday Surprise Notes:

This will kill any predictability your husband may think he knows about you. There is nothing wrong with creating moments the two of you can do something out of the box. Don't become so complacent in your marriage that you forget to play with each other. Keep learning each other; you never know what you might discover that could bring you all kinds of pleasure in more ways than one.

Nice – Shower Together

Taking a shower together can really be an innocent task that offers you intimacy you didn't think you needed. There must be some places you can't reach. Make it a regular practice to shower together or at least a few days a week and especially on weekends. It's not easy getting up most mornings, but if you whisper in her ear that it was time to get up and that you need her to wash your back or vice versa maybe it will give them the motivation they need to rise and shine. The intimacy this brings is so special. You're with each other at you're most vulnerable. Naked! Flaws and all!

If the shower isn't big enough for the both of you, then be there waiting for them with a towel for them to dry off and proceed to help them dry off. When everyone is all dry, don't forget that last butt pat to send them on their way to finish their morning adulations before getting dressed for work. This will lead to the start of a great day!

Shower Together Notes:

No hiding yourself, ladies. Embrace yourself, so your man can as well. Nothing is more frustrating than someone having to convince you that you're beautiful. You must believe it without someone having to tell you that you are. Fearfully and wonderfully made is what we all are, and everyone is not meant to be the same size. How boring would life be if everyone one looked alike, the uniqueness that God has given us alone makes us special and one of a kind. Even identical twins have differences that set them apart. Love yourself and the way God made you.

Nice – Cook A Meal Together

There is nothing sexier than a man in the kitchen. Make it fun and sexy. You've both arrived home from work and settling in for the evening. After changing into more comfortable clothes, you both make your way into the kitchen. Walk up to him and let him know that for dinner tonight you're going to need his help. This will probably surprise him, especially if he's not that good in the kitchen. Slide your arms around him and let him know that you're going to guide him through it all and seal it with a soft kiss on the lips. To help eliminate his worries let him know that you've had a home meal kit delivered with all of the ingredients and the recipe so it's as simple as following instructions. As he's opening the kit and pulling out the ingredients go and turn off all of the lights in the other parts of the house and turn on some soft music (jazz, classical, whatever you'd prefer) and set the table and make sure you add candles. He may be skeptical but give him a nice reassuring rub across his back and slide your hand down low to his nice tushy and give a light pat and let him know just how sexy it is to see him in the kitchen and lean in for another soft kiss. Once all of the ingredients are out of the box, along with the recipe and instructions, let him read them and you verify that all of the needed ingredients are present and then you begin to search for the pot and pans you're going to need and utensils. Make sure you're brushing up against him as much as possible. A little stimulation for the rest of the evening is always nice. As you begin pulling the meal together per the recipe, move the conversation to topics about your relationship. Let him know that you appreciate him and all that he does for you. Men need to hear this and know that we're not taking them protecting and caring for us for granted. Cooking together can be intimate and fun and it can be a relaxed way to communicate with one another. The task of cooking is distracting enough to where neither of you will probably realize how much fun you're having and it's a way to get to know each other as you're growing in your relationship. Who's to say you can't fall in love again over a meal. Even if you begin to reminisce about how you met and all that you've gone through to be together. It's good to be reminded that it may not have always been easy, but you've made it. This creates several moments for kisses. Remember, don't burn the food, you still need to eat and let's not forget the dessert, chocolate fudge and your husband is always a nice treat, or you can share a bowl of ice cream.

Cook A Meal Together Notes:

Remember this can be done in reverse if she's not the best cook then men take over. And if neither of you can cook, imagine the fun you can have just trying, but keep the pizza place on speed dial, just in case. This is such a good way to relax with each other. That may be a strange statement to make, but couples can drift a part because of the different obstacles or challenges life throws at them and before you know it you don't know the person you're lying next to at night. You're sharing your lives with each other and it's important to remain connected. So, go online and have a meal kit delivered and rediscover why you fell in love in the first place. There are so many options to choose from, "Hello Fresh", "Home Chef", "Sun Basket", "Plated", etc.

NICE – HOLDING HANDS

For men this may sound elementary, but it's such a loving small gesture for her. Holding her hand as you stroll along to wherever it may be, means much. It's the skin to skin contact, the sheer warmth of your touch, the connection it offers is what she loves. The simple fact that you're holding her hand in public has significant meaning to a woman. It's as if you're staking your claim and saying without words, "She's mine." Holding her hand and showing others, as her man, you don't care who's watching, she's your main concern. How can something so simple, say so much? Think about it, if you're holding her hand your leading her and guiding her where you want her to be and all this keeps her by your side. When woman was created it was from the side of man, so it's only fitting that you keep her there with this very simple gesture. You're saying a lot, without having to say anything. The old statement, "Your actions speaks louder than your words," rings true in this case.

Holding Hands Note:

Think of it like this, when you were only boyfriend and girlfriend you made it a point to give each other little touches here and there. Being embarrassed by PDA didn't even cross your mind. To reach for her hand was an action you didn't even think about because you wanted the connection and you wanted to make the statement that she was yours. Keep thinking of her as your girlfriend and just automatically reach for her hand. And if you want more brownie points, offer her your arm to hold, this one will definitely get your wife to smile and gush like she did when she was your girlfriend. Besides, it was the actions of the boyfriend that made her fall in love in the first place. So, make it a point to do this, because it's the small gestures that women look for and they go a long way.

Fun and Naughty – Game Night (Strip Connect 4)

Game night is always full of fun, now it can be naughty too. Pull out the Connect 4 game and lay out the rules. Whoever connects 4 of their color in a row, in any direction, the other player will be required to discard an article of clothing. This can be so much fun and imagine the heat it will create between you and your partner, as you're peeling away your clothing piece by piece. This game play will not only make you laugh, but it will also turn you on. To kick it up a notch the person who wins each game gets to pick the piece of clothing that must be removed. Here's a stipulation, you can't ask for her bra if she's still wearing the shirt or dress. Don't forget ladies', men wear far fewer articles of clothing than we do, so you must try your best to win as many games as possible to be able to sit there and watch all his glory for your eyes to see now and hands to explore, later. Make it sexier by playing some music to match the mood the game has created, and this will also make removing each item of clothing feel like a strip tease. And it's okay to tell them to remove it slowly, to heighten the sexual tension. Remember, the object of the game is to get one of you completely naked. The first to get the other naked is the winner of Game Night in more ways than one. Now you can collect your prize and remember why you were created to love each other…

Game Night Notes:

If Connect 4 isn't your game, then this will work with any game you chose, but make sure it's for 2 players only. Pick a game that doesn't take all night to finish, because you will kill the fun of stripping or the mood all together.

Naughty, Nice, & Spicy – Husband Appreciation Day

Husband Appreciation Day is a day you will set aside just to celebrate and love on him. Go all out and make sure he doesn't have anything planned for that day. As a matter of fact, block his calendar for that day so he can't schedule anything. To insure he doesn't try to make any plans on this day, let him know that you have something special planned for him that will take the entire day and not to worry he will enjoy it. If you have children, plan for them to stay with your parents, trusted friend or family member.

Treat the day as if it's Valentine's Day just for him. First, tell him how special he is and how amazing he has made your life. Even through hard times you stayed together and worked through them. Everyday isn't sunshine and rainbows, because life happens, but you've worked to make it work. In today's society where people use any excuse to separate or even go so far as to get a divorce, you're still together. If you don't know how to express what it is you'd like to say, try something like this,

> *"Today is the day I want to appreciate you for being the man in my life. Not only are you an answered prayer, you've been more than what I asked God for and whatever you want that I can do or provide it's yours. I've learned that it doesn't take a lot to express*

my love for you, because you make loving you so easy.
So, my Love, this day is all about you."

Start the day off with a nice morning treat by waking him with kisses all over his face and then kiss your way down his body and kiss him in his special place, until he can't remember his name. Don't rush take your time and do it right. Remember he deserves it. Now that he's awake (or possibly ready to go back to sleep), proceed to let him know that today is Husband Appreciation Day and that the entire day is for him. So, if he needs a little nap after your morning delight then let him take one. If not, proceed with the morning.

When he's ready, lead him to the bathroom and while he's taking care of his morning adulations, get the shower ready. When he's ready for the shower, help him remove his pajamas. (If he's wearing any after your special kiss.) Then step back and allow him to get in the shower first and then you join him and let him know that you're going to bathe him, and he can return the favor. We already know what this will lead to, so have fun in the shower, because the day is just getting started. Once you've steamed up the bathroom with your shared shower, then step out and wrap a towel around you and then take a nice fluffy towel and then proceed to dry him from the top of his head to his feet. Then, where ever you get dressed lead him there and help him lotion down his body. After, let him finish his morning routine to get dressed, but tell him to keep his attire comfortable for the time being. Let him know that he can climb back in bed while you get his breakfast. You must get dressed but keep it light and sexy and since men are visual get dressed in front of him and make a big show of it.

While he's kicked back and relaxed you go prepare his favorite breakfast. (Or, you can choose to have someone else prepare breakfast.) Turn on some nice soothing music while the food is being prepared. Once breakfast is ready, let him choose if he wants to eat at the table or you serve him in bed. Make sure all of his favorite breakfast foods are there. This should lead to a very fun and exciting conversation about all that will take place for him that day. After you've finished breakfast, lead him to the family room to relax and do as he please until his lunchtime surprise arrives. Make sure you give him his gift with a card to show your love and appreciation. Make sure the gift is something he wants or has been hinting at getting for himself. This will show him that you do listen to him. While he's relaxing if that means he wants to play video games, then he can because it's his day and he can do and have whatever he likes. Even if that means he wants more of you. Make sure you wholeheartedly welcome that suggestion.

His next surprise should be mid-afternoon, so make sure he's dressed properly to venture outside. When the doorbell rings or there's a knock at the door, he sees his next surprise is a chauffeured limo that is ready to take him anywhere he'd like to go around town. It doesn't matter where, it's all about him. Let him shine and be the man, make him feel like he's the Man that he is by escorting him to the car and telling the driver your husband will instruct him on where he wants to go. Even if he just wants to ride around the town, it's up to him. Let him know he has the option to go by himself or you can join him. If he opts to take you with him show him how much fun, you can have in the back of the limo, soft kisses, light petting to name a few. Remember you're heading to a destination, so you can't get to carried away, just yet. After he's been taken to all of the places he wants to go, then let him know he has a dinner date with you at his favorite restaurant. The car returns you home from your afternoon excursion, so you both can refresh and change for your dinner date. Make sure you keep it sexy, pull out his favorite dress and pair it with your sexy heels.

What he doesn't know is you reserved the private room and filled it with balloons. The stand out are the balloons that spell out "I LOVE YOU" in giant gold balloons in the middle of the other cream and red balloons (or his favorite colors). The table is set in the middle of the room for just the two of you with low candles burning. You let him know that he can order whatever he wants from the menu.

Dinner conversation should be easy at this point and beautiful love ballads are playing softly in the background. Once dinner is finished let him know that dessert will be at home and explain that it's one of his favorites, because you should always be his ultimate favorite dessert. Lead him out of the restaurant and back to the waiting limo and instruct the driver to take you back home, but to take the scenic route. Since this is the ride home, it's no-holds barred in the back of the limo, use your imagination and do all of the naughty things you both thought about when you first got in the limo earlier in the day. If he wants to pleasure you then let him. If he wants you to pleasure him, then move between his thighs, unfasten his belt and pants, have him raise his hips so you can pull his pants down and then look him in his eyes as you take him into your hot mouth. And when he can't take the pleasure anymore, remove your panties (if you're wearing any) pull your dress up and straddle his lap and give him the ride of his life. Remember it's about his pleasure and not yours, take your pleasure from simply pleasing him. By the time he climaxes you've reached home. Ease up from his lap and right your clothing before exiting the limo. After stumbling into the house, you then began to remove his clothes and head to the bathroom for a nice shower where again you bathe him, and he gets to bathe you if he so chooses. After you're both nice and clean from getting dirty in the limo let him know the night isn't over, he still can do whatever his likes…

Husband Appreciation Day Notes:

This day should not just be done once, you should give him a day every year and change it up and keep him guessing. Have him excited about it each year. You can do this even if you're on a budget, it doesn't have to be about the expense. Some men like simple and some men would probably just want a day all to themselves and that is perfectly fine, let him do whatever he wants. It's all about letting him know you love him and that you want him to know just how much you appreciate the loving and caring man that he is and that regardless of the other women out there he has a woman at home who knows that he is great. Never give your man a reason to seek affection from someone else. Men need romance and love to, maybe not on the same level as a woman, but it's still needed. One thing I've learned is most men do not know how to articulate this fact, so you must be in tune with your man, so you can make sure you know when he needs that extra attention. If you have children, remember, they will grow up and leave one day, but your husband will remain, don't neglect him because of the children. Find the balance and keep home, just that home. A loving place that he can't wait to get back to each day.

Sweet and Nice – A Night to Remember

As a couple pick a night to sit down and reminisce about the day you met. Recount all of the nervous moments that they don't know about. Talk about how you got to where you are today in your relationship and how you knew they were the one. I would say, go far as to try to redo the first date all over again. Men, if you didn't have much money and couldn't afford to take her to some place fancy, take her back to that place, order the same food you ordered that night (if the place still exists). If you can't go back to the place it all started, then try to recreate the meal at home. If the place was inexpensive then it shouldn't be too hard to do.

Remembering helps you not forget how far you've grown in your love for each other. Talk about the good and bad, this will help you know not to do that again and laugh about some of the silly arguments you've had over the years. The surprising thing is you will find yourself falling in love with your husband or wife all over again.

A Night to Remember Notes:

If you communicate and share with each other even if you have to create an environment of comfort to do it in, then do it. You may save yourself some money from couples counseling. And if you do need couples counseling, there's nothing wrong with therapy, so you can find your way back to each other. Sometimes reminiscing can lead to a whole new beginning. Especially, when one or both of you see that you've dropped the ball in the relationship. Ladies, it's not always the man who's changed.

Nice and Slow –
Dance with Her

Although the thought of a slow dance may be a simple concept, it's such an intimate act. Women crave intimacy beyond sex. Think about it like this. You stand up in front of everyone. You walk up to her, hold out your hand, and lean in and ask her, "May I have this dance?" The joy she feels in that moment can't be expressed because she's trying to play down her excitement. This is a public display, saying you want her out of all the women in the room. The warmth of your hands connecting sends a tingling sensation of electricity flowing through her from her hand to the pit of her belly, it's so very exciting. The full effect of the slight pull, to help her to her feet, sends that current from the initial connection of your hands pass her belly to her intimate core. Being the man that you are, you lead her to the dance floor still holding her hand. Again, for all to see, you are there with her and her alone. This silent declaration is priceless for a woman and you seal your night when you pull her in close to you and gently embrace her and she rests her head upon your chest and close her eyes, as you glide your strong hands around her waist. This is exhilarating and so sexy. Her breast against your chest, thighs rubbing together, and you're slowly moving to the rhythm of not just the slow ballad, but the rhythm of the two of you. And you stay that way for the duration of the song. To top it off a nice kiss on the lips when it's over will be the icing on the cake.

This can also be done in the privacy of your own home. If you're on a budget, be spontaneous and turn on some music and go to her and ask her to just dance with you. Pull her up from her chair, sofa, or floor, wherever she is sitting and pull her into your strong embrace and because it's a private dance, your hands can go pass her waist and rest on her backside. A little squeeze in the process will only heighten the experience. Holding her this way also gives her a sense of safety. Women have an engrained need to feel protected and loved by her man and you've given her all of that without spending a dime.

Dance with Her Note:

Dancing is an act of intimacy, which women crave. The rhythm of the music moves you and it allows you to connect without words. Actions will always speak louder than words.

NICE AND NAUGHTY
COUPLE PAMPERING DAY

In relationships today, everyone is under some form of stress from their jobs or just life. Sometimes you just have to take the time to relax from it all. You work hard and deserve the best so plan a pamper day together.

Take an afternoon and have a light lunch and then have a couple's massage with a reputable spa. There are so many options that you can do together, such as fresh body scrubs, aromatherapy massages, spa pedicures, and even facials. Men, to ease your mind about the facial, know that it can help relieve razor burn. After your time at the spa, go to a nice dinner at your favorite restaurant, don't rush dinner, take your time. Return home and take a nice long bath together. He gets to bathe you and you get to bathe him and this can lead to a very exciting evening for you both. Let him help you rub on your body lotion and rub lotion on his hard to reach places, wherever they may be.

There is cost associated with this day, but if you plan, it will be worth the effort. You can use the time to reconnect, talk and share your thoughts and feelings with each other. Take the time to talk about the difficult things, sometimes a change in environment can make it easier to express yourself. Some spas even have suites, where you can spend the day or even the night if you choose.

Now, if your budget is unable to accommodate an actual spa you can turn your bedroom into a relaxing space. How? Set a day aside and turn your bedroom into your own personal spa space. Then turn the lights down low or light candles around the room and turn the lights off, turn on some soft jazz, love ballads, or soothing sounds (you can get these from YouTube) and use your smartphone or tablet as your radio. Make sure you have some baby oil or whatever you prefer to use as a lubricant (make sure to keep it in some warm water) as your massage oil. Then, prepare your bed as the massage table and pull the comforter and top sheet back only leaving the flat sheet and lay down some towels. (This is to keep the oil you use to massage with from getting on the flat sheet and ruining your mattress.) You will massage each other. Since it's just the two of you, do this naked. The warmth of your skin to skin contact will make the massage sweeter and sexier. Ladies, I would suggest you start first and have him lay on his front across the bed, put the warm oil nearby and climb up on him and straddle his waist, put some oil in your hands and begin working his back and rub up to his shoulders and keep doing this until you think it's time to move lower, but before you do make sure you add a little more oil and lean you entire body in and make sure he feels you. Flip your body around and straddle him again, this time facing his legs. Here's where it gets a little naughty. Make sure your intimate area is over his buttocks and then add more oil to your hands and begin to slowly massage his legs. Since the oil is warm you can even drizzle it on his legs and make sure you lean your body in, so he can feel all of you as you rub down his legs and then you will need to change positions again, flip back around facing his back, but settle on the back of his thighs. Take your warm oil and pour a small amount into your hands. This time your focus will be his gluteus maximus, yes, his buttocks. Gently, massage this area and more likely than not, he's going to need to turn over. And since you're not in a professional setting, there is nothing wrong with giving him an extremely happy ending. Make sure you have a warm extra hand towel to help with clean up. (Wink). Then it's his turn to give you a full body rub down. Of course, he may not be able to put his full weight on you, but he may be able to straddle the backs of your legs and put most of his weight on his knees. Using the warm oil, he can rub you from your neck down to your gluteus maximus and gently knead. Afterwards he can shift to the side of you and rub down the backs of your legs and then ease your legs apart slightly and rub up your inner thighs gently kneading along the way. Now, don't be surprised, but this will probably elicit a moan and the need to turn over. After shifting to your back, he will need more oil, but I would like to suggest that he move in between your legs to make it easier to rub your upper body. He can then drizzle some of the warm oil on your chest area. Yes, he's in a very delicious position, but remember this is a personal massage. Let him continue rubbing the oil on your chest and gently rubbing your breasts and then sliding down to your tummy and easing back so he can properly rub your hips and after making his way down to your toes he will make his way slowly back up to your inner thighs and then add more warm oil to you very sensitive core. This is where it's going to get extremely naughty. Now, it's your turn to receive your own happy ending. Men remember this area is sensitive and be gentle. The gentler you are the more responsive and pleased she's going to be. Rub the lips of her core first and then begin rubbing her pearl slowly and the more you rub the more responsive and then she too will climax from your masterful hands.

Couple Pamper Day Notes:

Doing this to each other shows how selfless you can be for the other. It's not about his or her pleasure alone, it's about sharing the pleasure together. And by doing this in the privacy of your own home you can schedule this anytime you'd like. It can be done after the children have been put to bed so no need for a sitter. If you're able to set aside funds for this day, then make sure you enjoy all of the amenities the spa can offer a couple.

SWEET AND NAUGHTY – MEN LET HER HEAR YOU

Let her hear you. It was your words when you approached her that got her attention. It didn't matter that the line was cheesy, it was the fact that you got the nerve to say it and that is what got her attention. It's funny how some men think they have to come up with some elaborate line to get a woman's attention, but a sweet, "Hello", can get you further. Hearing you talk about what made you approach her is also a nice boost to her ego and it's good for her self-esteem. This boost tells her that you thought she was worth ignoring all of the other women in the room to come and talk with her. Women need to hear you express yourself. When you can talk sweet and naughty it's oh, so, sexy. Call her during the day just to tell her, she was on your mind. And this will keep you on her mind all day long. Hearing you keeps her connected to you and no other man can get in her head, because your voice has taken up residence. The saying, "Men fall for what they see and women for what they hear," has been proven more times than not. There are so many ways to communicate now, this can be done either verbally, through text messaging, or a song if you can't get the words out. Naughty talk can be so fun, tell her what you're going to do to her when you see her or what you want her to do to you. Ask her questions that will make her blush. You don't have to be too vulgar or you can, know your wife so you don't get into trouble. The thought of your husband expressing his desire for you can be a turn on and a start of the fun to come. Ask her out of nowhere, "What color are your panties?" Then proceed to tell her why that color is your favorite and how you plan to take them off of her. Preferably with your teeth. Or even better tell her to take them off and give them to you. Describe in very explicit details why you love looking at her and tell her how you like tasting her all over. For women it's as important to reach her mentally as well as physically. The more you have her mind the easier it is to get her to climax when the time comes. How? Because you've been in her head all day. This is another reason why women like communication and it keeps your connection solid.

Men Let Her Hear You Notes:

The more she hears you the more in tune the two of you will be within your relationship. Women understand and know that men don't care to talk, but the communication factor is still key for any relationship to withstand the ups and downs of life. Even if you have to take baby steps start somewhere and watch the difference in your relationship. Women, listen, don't just wait to talk, because by not relating to him about what he's saying will only cause him to shutdown again and no one knows how long it will be before he tries to open up again.

NICE LEADS TO NAUGHTY –
FOOT RUB FOR HIM

There is nothing wrong with giving your man a foot massage. This is a nice way to combine two things. A pedicure and foot massage. I suggest doing this on a day when he's had a tough day at work and needs to relax. Remember this is for him and not about you. Let him get comfortable and serve him dinner. There is nothing wrong with serving your man, let me interject that here. He's the head of the house, provider, and protector of the family. He's entitled to some pampering just for him. Once he's changed into some comfortable clothes and he's full, let him know to go into the family room and relax you're going to come and give him a foot massage. Put some warm water and some Calgon salts into the foot basin (or use whatever you have in your home that is wide enough for him to place both feet in at the same time). Make sure to put a towel under the basin to catch any water that may spill out while you pamper your man. Keep another large towel nearby to dry his feet as well and some warm baby oil to massage his feet. (keep the baby oil in some warm water nearby) After he's soaked in the warm water for several minutes or until the water begins to cool, have him lift his feet out move the basin and let him rest his feet on the towel under the basin and then take the water and change it with some clean warm water and grab your puma stone to give him a quick pedicure. Examine his feet and if he needs his toenails clipped do that as well. If you notice he feet need more attention, then get your puma stone out and proceed to remove the excess skin from his feet. Once that is complete then move the basin back under his feet, so he can rinse them again. After rinsing them have him lift his feet so you can move the water again and place his feet back on the towel. Dispose of the water in the basin and return to finish drying his feet with the extra towel, take your time and gently rub each. While drying his feet ask him about his day. Now, he may want to talk, and he may not, it's his prerogative. If he says he doesn't want to talk about it, then let him know it's okay and turn on some soft music and tell him to lean back and let you take care of him. Once his feet are dry use the warm baby oil and begin massaging his feet. Take your time and give him your complete attention. Once you're done, maneuver up between his legs on your knees and let him know how much you love him and ask if he needs anything else to help him relax. I'm sure he will be able to think of something. Have fun and cherish your man...

Foot Rub for Him Note:

Men don't really require a lot of attention, but they do need some attention. If he's having a rough week or day, show him in some small way that the world outside your home may be rough at times, but the love you have together at home can melt all of that stress away with a little tender loving care from his wife.

NICE – LET HER TALK

This one may be a hard one for men, but it's a sweet gesture for her. Sometimes women really need to talk, and they want you to hear them. Remove distractions, turn off the TV, if you have kids send them to their rooms or go into your bedroom. Don't see this as a moment of torture for you, but as chance to let the woman you've made your wife have some inner peace. Women keep a lot inside, trying to be strong for everyone. Women would like to take the Superwoman cape and suit off and just be. And as her husband, you are the one person she needs to be able to be weak in front of. The talk may not even last long and ladies this is not about bashing your husband this is about expressing your feelings as the grown woman you are and needing him to understand your needs and frustrations. This is about being heard. At times during discussions women feel as if they're not being heard. She's not asking you to solve anything and as a man your natural instincts kick-in and say, "fix it". Well, not in this case.

Simply listen.

You may even feel like her thoughts aren't valid but understand to her they are. Feelings are not something you can fix or change within her, she needs to discuss it and hash it out for herself. Most times, if women can discuss it, then they can have clarity on the entire situation. This also may bring on tears and a lot of men can't handle seeing their women cry but know this is a cleansing cry and when the time comes gently pull her into your arms and hold her. When she's all cried out, let her relax while you get a warm face towel, for her to wash her face and take this time to simply cuddle. Hold her and let her know you're there for her to listen whenever she needs you. This is how being her best friend makes listening to her easier, because friends are always there for each other and listen to one another. Letting her talk doesn't have to be the punishment most men assume it is, sometimes, she just wants to vent and as her husband it's your job to be there to listen and comfort her. Again, this is very important, don't offer any solutions, just listen to her pour out her heart. Only make a suggestion if she asks, if she doesn't ask then leave her alone until she does.

Let Her Talk Notes:

Men usually cringe when they hear, "I need to talk," from their woman. It doesn't have to be all dramatic, it usually gets dramatic when the man displays his desire not to want to hear her. Women respond to this in anger (bringing on more drama), when it's more of the fact that her feelings her hurt. She expects her man to listen, meaning pay attention and hear, which means receive what she is saying. This is a simple way to make her happy.

NICE DAY AWAY – ALONE

A day is going to come where your significant other just needs some alone time.

Give it to them.

You may be surprised and realize you need some alone time yourself. This doesn't mean your relationship is over or he or she doesn't love you any more (stop being dramatic), it simply means they would like to do the things they enjoy doing without being concerned if you're enjoying yourself or not.

Ladies it can be freeing to go shopping without looking at your watch to make sure you don't spend too much time in the store because your husband hates when you take your time looking at bedding. While he stands around looking lost. Yes, this is boring to a man, but it's enjoyable to a woman because a woman is imagining what the room is going to look like once she's changed the bedding. Then she's anticipating her husbands' reaction to the change and hoping he's going to love it as much as she does. When, spoiler alert, he really doesn't care about the bedding as long as he can get some sleep and good loving in it, he could care less. Sorry, but it's true.

He could want to go to a sporting event with a group of friends, without worrying about if his wife is ready to go or him having to censor his conversation because she may not like the joke he's telling or he can't get into the game because he's having to explain too many aspects of the game (for this he could have stayed home). This may not be the case for all women, because some do like sports, it can just be more fun with the guys. Ladies, giving him a little time to himself, also it shows how secure you are in trusting that your man will return to you unscathed. Being in a relationship can be taxing enough at times with life attacking you. So, giving each other space every once in a while, doesn't hurt anyone and you get to have some alone time too. No worrying, just relaxing and enjoying your own company.

Alone Note:

Your husband or wife will appreciate you for giving them time to do what they like to do, whatever that may be.

Nice, Naughty, and Sweet Fantasy – Goodnight Baby

"Goodnight Baby", and he leans over and says the same, but he turns over onto his side. His back is to me and my back is to him, how do I communicate to him that I'm simply laying here craving his touch. How do I get him to understand that I want to feel the warmth of his body against mine? All of this is going through my mind as I breathe in his essence. He's mine and I'm his, why can't I just let him know that I want him. Will he be receptive to me taking the role as the initiator? He smells so delicious from his shower. So, I turn over to face him and lift the covers slightly, so I can slide up behind him. I position myself in spoon fashion on him and then place my arm over his hip and ease my leg between his, as I kiss the back of his neck and tell him how much I need to feel him, all of him. He then turns to me and pulls me in for a kiss that is so sweet and tender that it makes me want to weep, then he kisses my eyes, the tip of my nose, then again gently on my lips and when I sigh into his mouth he gently eases his tongue between my lips and our tongues meet and its heaven. The slow drugging way he kisses me makes me melt into him. I'm so engulfed in his kiss that I don't even register him easing me onto my back and my body automatically spreads for him to lay between my legs. I can now feel the weight of his body pressing me into the bed. It feels so divine, it's an answer to my silent prayer and so much more. He breaks the kiss which makes me groan and eases to his knees and smiles down at me to instruct me to remove my sleeper tank. I quickly disperse the tank and watch as his eyes light up to seeing my exposed breasts that are tightening just from his heated gaze. My God I love this man. He then takes his strong warm hands and begins to massage my breasts. I love it when he does this, he's so gentle. He flattens his hands and rubs in a circular motion until my nipples are so hard they ache, and I arch my back as an offering to him to place his hot mouth on them. His form of torture is so invigorating. Before he lets me feel the wonder of his tongue on them, he used his forefinger and thumb of each hand and gently squeezes my nipples so a shot of electricity zips down my belly to my groin and this causes my hips to rise and sway and I reach up to pull him to me for another toe-curling kiss. He knows at this point I have to feel his lips on my nipple, so I break the kiss and release his head and offer him my right nipple to suckle and he gives me his cocky smile and lowers his head and takes my breast into his hand, squeezes and gives my nipple a swipe of his tongue before pulling it into his hot wet mouth and suckling like it's his first time. And he uses his other hand to worry my left nipple until he feels like it needs some attention too. This is driving me to climax and he knows it because he knows my body. While paying homage to my left breast his other hand has made its way into my panties and he finds me so wet that he just eases one of his fingers inside of me, in and out, in and out until I scream out his name from the explosion that takes my breath away. He lifts his head from my chest and takes his finger that just gave me an amazing orgasm and sucks it into his mouth. I feel my body heat up all over again just from watching him taste me from his finger. He removes his tank and briefs and takes his engorged sex in his hand and as he's kneeling in front of me he begins to stroke himself. This is so hot. I sit up and remove his hand and replace it with mine. He feels so hard and velvety smooth. He throws his head back and I love the feeling it gives me to know that I can make him this turned on, this needy for me and only me. I lean in more and kiss the tip and release him to lay back down and open my legs wider because at this moment

I need to feel his power, his strength, and him stretching me to fit around his gorgeous member knowing my body was design just for him. As he begins to come down on me to penetrate my core, I tell him, "Do it slow, Baby, I want to feel every inch of you." He gives me that cocky grin again and slowly begins to enter, it's so exquisite that I close my eyes, flex my vaginal muscles and purr his name. When he's fully sheathed in my body and begins his slow grind I hear the sweet music of our souls connecting on a level no man can touch but us. It's a song that only he can play, and I love it when he turns the music up when he tells me to open my eyes because he wants me to see him loving me. When I open my eyes and see the love he has for me shining and unashamed, I come, and I come again. My body seems to be shaking uncontrollably. He's still slow grinding, until I tell him, "faster, Baby." He picks up the pace and leans in and I feel him expand more inside me and then he takes my mouth and duals with my tongue and releases his seed into my womb and I wrap my arms around him and run my hands up and down his sweaty back and bask in the love we have for each other. I enjoy his weight as he continues to kiss me and then he releases my mouth and we shift in unison to a spooning position and he pulls me in and kisses my neck and I can feel his warm breath against my skin and it makes me smile and I push my tush into his groin and before I slip into a blissful sleep reserved for lovers, my final thoughts as I rest my arm on top of his is, Oh how I love this man.

Goodnight Baby Notes:

Couples can forget the intimacy and sweetness of that saying goodnight can be. The fantasy is only an idea to show you how sweet it can be, if one of you gives in and just go for it. She's wanting his touch, he's wanting her touch, but neither taking the chance to just ease in. Touch is important, don't go a day without touching each other, this keeps the love and affection alive in your relationship.

Nice and Naughty – Date Night

Life can often get in the way and sometimes you must remember to keep your relationship in the forefront, so you don't grow apart unknowingly, which means you must carve out time for your love.

Go on a lovely date, which should be a part of your routine to keep your intimate connection burning. Dating shouldn't just be a part of the courting phase. It should always be a part of your relationship. It's that part of getting to know each other and it's what made you fall in love in the first place. If you never dated, you would have never fell in love. When you knew you were going out with that special someone you always took extra care in your appearance and you made sure you looked your absolute best, you were open, and communication was flowing. This should never stop.

Men pick a restaurant that has good food and a romantic atmosphere. Ask for a quiet spot in the restaurant where you can sit side by side. Sitting across from each other doesn't allow for much physical contact or much play time, so you must sit beside each other and if you can sit in a booth that's even better. It offers a small amount of privacy, especially when your hands decide to roam a little. Okay, this is fun, but keep it between the lines because you are in public. There is something about being naughty in public that heightens the experience. Sit so close to where you're touching from your thighs to your shoulder. Sliding your hand up and down her thigh can send a delicious shiver over her body. Ladies, you can turn it up a notch and make him even hotter when you lean in and whisper you're not wearing any panties and make sure you kiss his ear before sitting back up and taking a sip of your drink. Explain as sweetly as possible that you didn't want anything to get in the way of any fun you decided to have. This could lead to all kinds of possibilities. Playing in the elevator or the car ride home just got more interesting.

As you place your order for your food make sure you order food that can be shared. Let her taste your dish using your fork, not only will she taste the food, but also you. After she takes the food from your fork, look her in the eyes and lick the fork after her, just so you can taste her. This can cause more shivers and you didn't even touch her. While you're eating take the time to share your food with each other. You eat from her fork and she eats from yours. Keep it light because you need to reserve your energy for later. Ladies be careful where you rub him under the table, I don't think you'd like the others in the restaurant to know exactly what you two have been up too.

Dinner is over, and you make your way to the car, as he seats you in the car, make sure he can see how your dress rides up your thighs before he closes the door. Once he's seated behind the wheel and drives off, turn the radio to a slow jam station and recline your seat and slide your dress up and let him run his hand up your warm thigh. The recline position gives him better access to your already wet sex. He can inhale the scent of your arousal. Make sure he keeps his eyes on the road, he has to please you without looking at you. This makes the experience even more exciting. You have to tell him everything your feeling and guide his hand just where you need his fingers to be, so they can properly rub your swollen clit. Try to hold off your climax ladies until your home or time it just as he pulls into the driveway. While you're trying to get your breathing under control, watch as he licks his fingers clean of your sweet juices. Which turns you on all over again and you sit your seat up and lean over to give him the sweetest tongue tangling kiss and let him know that it's your turn to rub him to climax, while sitting in the driveway...

Date Night Notes:

Be careful with this one, don't get in trouble in public and definitely wait until you've reached your destination before you touch him intimately, you do not want to cause an accident. Always date your spouse, as you get older people change and this is how you can keep learning about each other and you get to fall in love over and over again. This is also important for couples with children, because the children are going to grow-up and leave and its sad when couples have centered their lives around their children to the point where they no longer know each other.

NICE AND NAUGHTY –
LAZY/NAKED DAY

This day is a must and should be done often.

In relationships the husband and the wife are working to make life better and because of this scheduling time to just be lazy is a must. Ladies make sure the fridge is stocked and/or take-out menus are on ready, because you're planning a Lazy/Naked Day with your man, no one is going to work, and no one is doing anything strenuous for a full day. Turn the volume down on your cell phones and no Social Media. Let your parents and friends know that they are not to contact you unless it's an emergency. This day is just for the two of you. I say, make it a Saturday, it's the weekend and the perfect time to just be. Sleep-in, share brunch at home, either cook it together or order it in. Once brunch is done, shower together and make sure you wash his back and he wash yours. Dry each other off and then have fun putting lotion on each other. I'm sure the lotion can be a nice lubricant for all of the rubbing that will take place when you apply lotion to certain areas. Then go back into the bedroom and finish what you started in the shower. Remember this is not only Lazy Day but also Naked Day so the only thing you will need is a robe (from time to time). Make love as much as you want and because the fridge is stocked you can even carry the fun to the kitchen. Making love in the kitchen can be so sexy. So many possibilities and surfaces, the counter, the table, the island, or bent over the same surfaces so he can take you from behind. When you can move again (smile) take a long bath just to hold each other and talk. After your bath order in your dinner favorites and feed each other and even pull out a deck of cards to play poker to strip each other of your robes. A quick one hand game. You can spice it up by having the winner of the game perform a naughty task just to keep it interesting. For example, loser must do a striptease dance for the winner.

Lazy/Naked Day Notes:

Stay on the same page in your marriage, take this time to reconnect and share what's on your mind. If taking a day in the middle of the week to have this fun is what you need to do, then do it. Break up the normal routine and add a little spice to Wednesday. Couples can also take this time to plan your next date night or even a weekend getaway. For those of you who have children let them stay with their grandparents or a trusted family member or friend. I'm sure you have a friend who owes you a favor. Always, think of ways to stay connected.

LAST THOUGHTS

Fight to stay connected, there are so many obstacles that will come to try to destroy what you have, but if you keep it interesting and keep other people out, you will not fail. My parents have been married for over 40 years and they decided early in their marriage that he would keep his family out of their marriage and she would keep her family out of their marriage and if they failed they wouldn't have anyone to blame but themselves and if they make it then there is no one to praise.

Here's one more thing to think about that wasn't around 40 years ago and that's Social Media. They are entertaining accounts to have, but they have been a source of contention for many marriages. If you must be on Social Media sites, then lose the separate accounts and connect using a couple account. This keeps others up to date on you and your spouse and it shows your committed to your marriage and it's easier to reject unwanted connections and it will eliminate unnecessary contention. Being in love isn't always easy and life is full of ups and downs, but you can have a good marriage as long as you keep each other first and remember, marriage is two imperfect people trying to have a perfect relationship, as my father would say. People often think marriage means no sex, no fun, but it really doesn't have to be that way.

Open your imagination and enjoy each other.